Burgoyne's Surrender: An Oration Delivered On The One Hundredth Anniversary Of The Event

George William Curtis

In the interest of creating a more extensive selection of rare historical book reprints, we have chosen to reproduce this title even though it may possibly have occasional imperfections such as missing and blurred pages, missing text, poor pictures, markings, dark backgrounds and other reproduction issues beyond our control. Because this work is culturally important, we have made it available as a part of our commitment to protecting, preserving and promoting the world's literature. Thank you for your understanding.

BURGOYNE'S SURRENDER:

AN ORATION DELIVERED ON THE

ONE HUNDREDTH ANNIVERSARY OF THE EVENT,

OCTOBER 17, 1877,

AT SCHUYLERVILLE, N. Y.

By GEORGE WILLIAM CURTIS.

NEW YORK:
BAKER & GODWIN, PRINTERS,
No. 25 Park Row,
1877.

ORATION.

WITHIN the territory of New York, broad, fertile and fair, from Montauk to Niagara, from the Adirondacks to the bay, there is no more memorable spot than that on which we stand. Elsewhere, indeed, the great outlines of the landscape are more imposing, and on this autumnal day the parting benediction of the year rests with the same glory on other hills and other waters of the imperial State. Far above, these gentle heights rise into towering mountains; far below, this placid stream broadens and deepens around the metropolis of the continent into a spacious highway for the commerce of the world. Other valleys with teeming intervale and fruitful upland, rich with romantic tradition and patriotic story, filled like this with happy homes and humming workshops, wind through the vast commonwealth, ample channels of its various life; and town and city, village and hamlet, church and school, everywhere illustrate and promote the prosperous repose of a community great, intelligent and free. But this spot alone within our borders is consecrated as the scene of one of the decisive events that affect the course of history. There are deeds on which the welfare of the world seems to be staked; conflicts in which liberty is lost or won; victories by which the standard of human progress is full high advanced. Between sunrise and sunset, on some chance field the deed is done, but from that day it is a field enchanted. Imagination invests it with

"The light that never was on sea or land."

The grateful heart of mankind repeats its name; Heroism feeds upon its story; Patriotism kindles with its perennial fire. Such is the field on which we stand. It is not ours. It does not belong to New York; nor to America. It is an indefeasible estate of the world, like the field of Arbela, of Tours, of Hastings, of Waterloo; and the same lofty charm that draws the pilgrim to the plain of Marathon resistlessly leads him to the field of Saratoga.

The drama of the revolution opened in New England, culminated in New York, and closed in Virginia. It was a happy fortune that the three colonies which represented the various territorial sections of the settled continent were each in turn the chief seat of war. The common sacrifice, the common struggle, the common triumph, tended to weld them locally, politically and morally together. Doubtless there were conflicts of provincial pride and jealousy and suspicion. The Virginia officers smiled loftily at the raw Yankee militia; the Green Mountain boys distrusted the polished discipline of New York; and the New York Schuyler thought those boys brave but dangerously independent. In every great crisis of the war, however, there was a common impulse and devotion, and the welfare of the continent obliterated provincial lines. It is by the few heaven-piercing peaks, not by the confused mass of upland, that we measure the height of the Andes, of the Alps, of the Himalaya. It is by Joseph Warren not by Benjamin Church, by John Jay not by Sir John Johnson, by George Washington not by Benedict Arnold, that we test the quality of the revolutionary character. The voice of Patrick Henry from the mountains answered that of James Otis by the sea. Paul Revere's lantern shone through the valley of the Hudson, and flashed along the cliffs of the Blue Ridge. The scattering volley of Lexington Green swelled to the triumphant thunder of Saratoga, and the reverberation of Burgoyne's falling arms in New York shook those of Cornwallis in Virginia from his hands. Doubts, jealousies, prejudices, were merged in one common devotion. The union of the colonies to secure liberty, foretold the union of the States to maintain it, and wherever we stand on revolutionary fields, or inhale the sweetness of revolutionary memories, we tread the ground and breathe the air of invincible national union.

Our especial interest and pride, to-day, are in the most important event of the revolution upon the soil of New York. Concord and Lexington, Bunker Hill and Bennington, the Brandywine and Germantown, have had their fitting centennial commemorations, and already at Kingston and Oriskany, New York has taken up the wondrous tale of her civil and military achievements. In proud continuation of her story we stand here. Sons of sires who bled with Sterling on the Long Island shore; who fought with Herkimer in the deadly Oneida defile; who defended the Highland forts with George Clinton; who, with Robert Livingston and Gouverneur Morris, were driven from town to town by stress of war, yet framed a civil constitution, all untouched by the asperity of the conflict and a noble model for all free States; sons of sires who, leaving the plough and the bench, gathered on this historic war-path—the key of the then civilized continent; the western battle ground of Europe; the trail by which Frontenac's Indians prowled to Schenectady, and crept to the Connecticut and beyond; the way by which Sir William Johnson and his army passed in the old French war, and humbled Dieskau at Lake George; the road along which Abercrombie and his bright array marched to disaster in the summer morning, and Amherst marshaled his men to co-operate with Wolf in the humbling of Quebec; sons of sires who, mustering here on ground still trembling with the tread of armies, where the air forever echoes with the savage warwhoop, or murmurs with the pathetic music of the march and the camp—

> "Why, soldiers, why
> Should we be melancholy, boys?
> Whose business 'tis to die!"

even here withstood the deadly British blow and enveloping the haughty Burgoyne, compelled not only him to yield his sword, but England to surrender an empire; sons of such sires, who should not proudly recall such deeds of theirs and gratefully revere their memory, would be forever scorned as faithless depositaries of the great English and American tradition, and the great human benediction, of patient, orderly, self-restrained liberty.

When King George heard of the battle of Bunker Hill, he consoled himself with the thought that New York was still unswervingly loyal; and it was the hope and the faith of his ministry that the rebellion might at last be baffled in that great colony. It was a region of vast extent, but thinly peopled, for the population was but little more than one hundred and sixty thousand. It had been settled by men of various races, who, upon the sea shore, and through the remote valleys, and in the primeval wilderness, cherished the freedom that they brought and transmitted to their children. But the colony lacked that homogeneity of population which produces general sympathy of conviction and concert of action; which gives a community one soul, one heart, one hand, interprets every man's thought to his neighbor, and explains so much of the great deeds of the Grecian commonwealths, of Switzerland, and of Old and New England. In New York, also, were the hereditary manors— vast domains of a few families, private principalities, with feudal relations and traditions—and the spirit of a splendid proprietary life was essentially hostile to doctrines of popular right and power. In the magnificent territory of the Mohawk and its tributaries, Sir William Johnson, amid his family and dependents, lived in baronial state among the Indians, with whom he was allied by marriage, and to whom he was the vicar of their royal father over the sea. The Johnsons were virtually supréme in the country of the Mohawk, and as they were intensely loyal, the region west of Albany became a dark and bloody ground of civil strife. In the city of New York, and in the neighboring counties of Westchester upon the river and sound, of Richmond upon the bay, and Queens and Suffolk on the sea, the fear that sprang from conscious exposure to the naval power of Great Britain, the timidity of commercial trade, the natural loyalty of numerous officers of the crown, all combined to foster antipathy to any disturbance of that established authority which secured order and peace.

But deeper and stronger than all other causes was the tender reluctance of Englishmen in America to believe that reconciliation with the mother country was impossible. Even after the great day on Bunker Hill, when, in full sight of his country and of all future America, Joseph Warren, the well-beloved disciple of American liberty, fell, Congress, while justifying war, recoiled from declaring independence. Doubtless the voice of John Adams, of Massachusetts, counseling immediate and entire separation, spoke truly for the unanimous and fervent patriotism of New England; but doubtless, also, the voice of John Jay, of New York, who knew the mingled sentiment of the great province whose position in the struggle must be decisive, in advising one more appeal to the king, was a voice of patriotism as pure, and of courage as unquailing.

The appeal was made, and made in vain. The year that opened with Concord and Lexington, ended with the gloomy tragedy of the Canada campaign. On the last day of the year, in a tempest of sleet and snow, the combined forces of New England and New York made a desperate, futile onset; and the expedition from which Washington and the country had anticipated results so inspiring was dashed in pieces against the walls of Quebec. The country mourned, but New York had a peculiar sorrow. Leaving his tranquil and beautiful home upon this river, one of her noblest soldiers—brave, honorable, gentle—the son in law of Livingston, the friend of Schuyler, after a brief career of glory, died the death of a hero. "You shall not blush for your Montgomery," he said to his bride, as he left her. For fifty years a widow, his bride saw him no more. But while this stately river flows through the mountains to the sea, its waves will still proudly murmur the name, and recall the romantic and heroic story of Richard Montgomery.

The year 1776 was not less gloomy for the American cause. Late in November Washington was hurriedly retreating across New Jersey, pursued by Cornwallis, his army crumbling with every step, the State paralyzed with terror,

Congress flying affrighted from Philadelphia to Baltimore, and the apparent sole remaining hope of American Independence, the rigor of winter, snow, and impassable roads. Ah, no! It was not in winter but in summer that that hope lay, not in the relentless frost of the elements, but in the heavenly fire of hearts beating high with patriotic resolve, and turning the snow flakes of that terrible retreat into immortal roses of victory and joy. While Howe and his officers, in the warm luxury and wild debauchery of the city they had captured, believed the war ended, gaily sang and madly caroused, Washington, in the dreary Christmas evening, turned on the ice of the Delaware, and struck the Hessians fatally at Trenton; then in the cold January sunrise, defeating the British at Princeton, his army filed with bleeding feet into the highlands of New Jersey, and, half starved and scantily clothed, encamped upon the frozen hills of Morristown. "The Americans have done much," said despairingly one of their truest friends in England, Edmund Burke, "but it is now evident that they cannot look standing armies in the face." That, however, was to be determined by the campaign of 1777.

For that campaign England was already preparing. Seven years before, General Carleton, who still commanded in Canada, had proposed to hold the water line between the Gulf of St. Lawrence and the bay of New York, to prevent a separation of the colonies. It was now proposed to hold it to compel a separation. The ocean mouths of the great waterway were both in complete possession of the crown. It was a historic war path. Here had raged the prolonged conflict between France and England for the control of the continent, and in fierce war upon the waters of New York, no less than on the plains of Abraham, the power of France in America finally fell. Here, also, where it had humbled its proud rival, the strong hand of England grasping for unjust dominion was to be triumphantly shaken off. This region was still a wilderness. Seventy years before, the first legal land title in it was granted. In 1745, thirty years before the Revolution, it was the extreme English outpost. In 1777, the settlers were few, and they feared the bear and the catamount less than the Tory and the Indian. They still built block houses for retreat and defense like the first New England settlers a hundred and fifty years before. Nowhere during the Revolution were the horrors of civil war so constant and so dire as here. The Tories seized and harassed, shot and hung the Whigs, stole their stock and store, burned their barns and ruined their crops, and the Whigs remorselessly retaliated. The stealthy Indian struck, shrieked and vanished. The wolf and the wild cat lurked in the thicket. Man and beast were equally cruel. Terror overhung the fated region, and as the great invasion approached, the universal flight and devastation recalled the grim desolation in Germany during the thirty years' war.

Of that invasion, and of the campaign of 1777, the central figure is John Burgoyne. No name among the British generals of the Revolution is more familiar, yet he was neither a great soldier nor a great man. He was willing to bribe his old comrade in arms, Charles Lee, to betray the American cause, and he threatened to loose savages upon the Americans for defending it. Burgoyne was an admirable type of the English fashionable gentleman of his day. The grandson of a baronet, a Westminster boy, and trained to arms, he eloped with a daughter of the great Whig house of Derby, left the army and lived gaily on the continent. Restored to a military career by political influence, he served as a captain in France, and returning to England was elected to Parliament. He went a brigadier to Portugal, and led a brilliant charge at Valentia d'Alcantara, was complimented by the great Count Lippe, and flattered by the British prime minister. For his gallantry the king of Spain gave him a diamond ring, and with that blazing on his finger he returned once more to England, flushed with brief glory. There for some years he was a man of pleasure. He wrote slight verses and little plays that are forgotten. Reynolds painted his portrait in London, as Ramsay had painted it in Rome. Horace Walpole sneered at him for his plays, but Lord Chatham praised him for his military notes. Tall and handsome, graceful and winning in manner, allied to a noble house, a favorite at court and on parade, he was a gay companion at the table, the club and the theatre. The king admired his dragoons, and conferred upon him profitable honors, which secured to him a refined and luxurious life. In Parliament, when the American war began, Burgoyne took the high British ground, but with the urbanity of a soldier, and he gladly obeyed the summons to service in America, and sailed with Howe and Clinton on the great day that the British troops marched to Concord. He saw the battle of Bunker Hill, and praised the American courage and military ability, but was very sure that trained troops would always overcome militia. The one American whom he extolled was Samuel Adams. He thought that he combined the ability of Cæsar with the astuteness of Cromwell; that he led Franklin and all the other leaders, and that if his counsels continued to control the continent, America must be subdued or relinquished.

Burgoyne saw little actual service in this country until he arrived at Quebec on the 6th of May, 1777, as commander of the great enterprise of the year. The plan of campaign was large and simple. One expedition led by Burgoyne, was to force its way from Quebec to Albany, through the valley of the Hudson, and another, under St. Leger, was to push through the valley of the Mohawk, to the same point. At Albany they were to join General Howe, who would advance up the river from the bay. By the success of these combined operations, the British would command New York, and New England would be absolutely cut off. This last result alone would be a signal triumph. New England was the nest of rebellion. There were the fields where British power was first defied in arms. There were the Green Mountains from which Ethan Allen and his boys had streamed upon Ticonderoga. There was Boston bay where the tea had been scattered, and Narragansett bay where the Gaspe had been burned, and the harbors of Machias and of Newport, from which British ships had been chased to sea. There were Fanueil Hall and the town meeting. There was Boston, whose port had been closed—Boston with the street of the massacre—Boston, of which King George had bitterly said that he would "as lief fight the Bostonians as the French." There were the pulpits which preached what Samuel Adams called liberty, and Samuel Johnson sedition. The very air of New England was full of defiance. The woods rustled it, the waters murmured it, the stern heart of its rugged nature seemed to beat in unison with the stout heart of man, and all throbbed together with the invincible Anglo Saxon instinct of liberty. To cut off New England from her sisters—to seize and hold the great New York valleys of Champlain and the Hudson—was to pierce the heart of the rebellion, and to paralyze America. Here, then, was to be the crucial struggle. Here in New York once more the contest for the Western continent was to be decided. Burgoyne had airily said in London, that with an army of ten thousand men he could promenade through America, and now the brilliant gentleman was to make good his boast.

While he was crossing the ocean to begin his task, and when every possible effort should have been made by Congress to meet the ample and splendid preparations for the British invasion, wretched intrigues displaced General Schuyler in the northern department, and it was not until late in May that he was restored to the command. The peril was at hand, but it was impossible to collect men. By the end of June, the entire garrison of Ticonderoga and Fort Independence, the first great barrier against the advance of Burgoyne, consisted of twenty-five hundred continentals and nine hundred militia, barefooted and ragged, without proper arms or sufficient blankets, and lacking every adequate preparation for defense. But more threatening than all, was Sugar-loaf Hill, rising above Ticonderoga, and completely commanding the fort. General Schuyler saw it, but even while he pointed out the danger, and while General St. Clair, the Commandant of the post, declared that from the want of troops nothing could be done, the drums of Burgoyne's army were joyfully beating in the summer dawn; the bugles rang, the cannon thundered, the rising June sun shone on the scarlet coats of British grenadiers, on the bright helmets of German dragoons, and on burnished artillery and polished arms. There were more than seven thousand trained and veteran troops, besides Canadians and Indians. They were admirably commanded and equipped, although the means of land transport were fatally insufficient. But all was hope and confidence. The battle flags were unfurled, the word was given, and with every happy augury, the royal standard of England proudly set forward for conquest. On the 1st of July, the brilliant pageant swept up Lake Champlain, and the echoes of the mighty wilderness which had answered the guns of Amherst and the drum-beat of Montcalm, saluted the frigates and the gunboats that, led by a dusky swarm of Indians in bark canoes, stretched between the eastern shore, along which Riedesel and the Germans marched, and the main body advancing with Phillips upon the west. The historic waters of Champlain have never seen a spectacle more splendid than the advancing army of Burgoyne. But so with his glittering Asian hordes, two thousand years before, the Persian king advanced to Salamis.

At evening the British army was before Ticonderoga. The trained eye of the English engineers instantly saw the advantage of Sugar-loaf, the higher hill, and the rising sun of the 5th of July glared in the amazed eyes of the Ticonderoga garrison, on the red coats entrenched upon Sugar-loaf, with their batteries commanding every point within the fort, and their glasses every movement. Sugar-loaf had become Mount Defiance. St. Clair had no choice. All day he assumed indifference, but quietly made every preparation, and before dawn the next day he stole away. The moon shone, but his flight was undetected, until the flames of a fire foolishly set to a house suddenly flashed over the landscape and revealed his retreat. He was instantly pursued. His rear guard was overtaken, and by the valor of its fierce but hopeless fight gave an undying name to the wooded hills of Hubbardton.

Ticonderoga fell, and the morning of its fall was the

high hour of Burgoyne's career. Without a blow, by the mere power of his presence, he had undone the electric deed of Ethan Allen; he had captured the historic prize of famous campaigns. The chief obstruction to his triumphal American promenade had fallen. The bright promise of the invasion would be fulfilled, and Burgoyne would be the lauded hero of the war. Doubtless his handsome lip curled in amused disdain at the flying and frightened militia, plough boys that might infest but could not impede his further advance. His eager fancy could picture the delight of London, the joy of the clubs, of Parliament, of the King. He could almost hear the royal George bursting into the Queen's room and shouting, "I have beat all the Americans." He could almost read the assurance of the minister to the proud Earl, his father-in-law, that the king designed for him the vacant Red Ribbon. But his aspiring ambition surely anticipated a loftier reward— a garter, a coronet, and at last, Westminster Abbey and undying glory.

Ticonderoga fell, and with it, apparently, fell in Europe all hope of the patriot cause; and in America, all confidence and happy expectation. The tories were jubilant. The wavering Indians were instantly open enemies. The militia sullenly went home. The solitary settlers fled southward through the forests and over the eastern hills. Even Albany was appalled, and its pale citizens sent their families away. Yet this panic stricken valley of the upper Hudson was now the field on which, if anywhere, the cause was to be saved. Five counties of the State were in the hands of the enemy; three were in anarchy. Schuyler was at Fort Edward with scarcely a thousand men. The weary army of St. Clair, shrunken to fifteen hundred continentals, all the militia having dropped away, struggled for a week through the forest, and emerged forlorn and exhausted at the fort. Other troops arrived, but the peril was imminent. New York was threatened at every point, and with less than five thousand ill-equipped regulars and militia to oppose the victorious Burgoyne, who was but a single long day's march away, with only the forts and the boom and chain in the Highlands to stay Clinton's ascent from the bay, and only the little garrison at Fort Stanwix to withstand St. Leger, General Schuyler and the council of State implored aid from every quarter. A loud clamor, bred of old jealousy and fresh disappointment, arose against Schuyler, the commander of the Department, and St. Clair, the commander of the post. The excitement and dismay were universal, and the just apprehension was most grave. But when the storm was loudest it was pierced by the calm voice of Washington, whose soul quailed before no disaster: "We should never despair; our situation has before been unpromising and has changed for the better; so I trust it will be again." He sent Arnold to Schuyler, as an accomplished officer, familiar with the country. He urged the Eastern States to move to his succor. He ordered all available boats from Albany to New Windsor and Fishkill, upon the Hudson, to be ready for any part of his own army that he might wish to detach. While thus the Commander-in-Chief cared for all, each cared for itself. The stout-hearted George Clinton, and the Council of New York were thoroughly aroused and alert. Vermont called upon New Hampshire, and the White Mountains answered to the Green by summoning Stark and Whipple, who, gathering their men, hastened to the Hudson.

While this wild panic and alarm swept through the country, Burgoyne remained for a fortnight at the head of Lake Champlain. He, also, had his troubles. He was forced to garrison Ticonderoga from his serviceable troops. His Indian allies began to annoy him. Provisions came in slowly, and the first fatal weakness of the expedition was already betrayed in the inadequate supply of wagons and horses. But the neighboring tories joined him, and counting upon the terror that his triumphant progress had inspired, he moved at the end of July from Lake Champlain toward the Hudson. His march was through the wilderness which Schuyler had desolated to the utmost, breaking up the roads, choking with trees the navigable streams, destroying forage, and driving away cattle. But Burgoyne forced his way through, building forty bridges and laying a log-wood road for two miles across a morass. The confidence of triumph cheered the way. So sure was victory, that as if it had been a huge pleasure party, the wives of officers accompanied the camp, and the Baroness Riedesel came in a calash from Fort George to join her husband with Burgoyne. But before that slowly toiling army, the startled frontier country fled. Almost every patriot house west of the Green Mountains and north of Manchester was deserted. The Tories, proud of British protection, placed signs in their hats and before their doors, and upon the horns of their cattle, wearing the Tory badge, as Gurth wore the collar of Cedric the Saxon. To us the scene is a romantic picture. The scarlet host of Burgoyne flashes through the forest with pealing music; the soldiers smooth the rough way with roystering songs; the trains and artillery toil slowly on; the red cloud of savages glimmers on his skirts, driving before him farmers with wives and children, faint and sick with cruel apprehension, flying through a land of terror. To us, it is picture. But to know what it truly was, let the happy farmer on these green slopes and placid meadows, imagine a sudden flight to-night with all he loves from all he owns, struggling up steep hills, lost in tangled woods, crowding along difficult roads, at every step expecting the glistening tomahawk, the bullet, and the mercies of a foreign soldiery. Not many miles from this spot, the hapless Jane Mac Crea was killed as Burgoyne's savages hurried her away. Her story rang through the land like a woman's cry of agony. This, then, was British chivalry! Burgoyne, indeed, had not meant murder, but he had threatened it. The name of the innocent girl became the rallying cry for armies, and to a thousand indignant hearts, her blood cried from the ground for vengeance. We come with song and speech and proud commemoration to celebrate the triumph of this day. Let us not forget the cost of that triumph, the infinite suffering that this unchanging sky beheld; the torture of men; the heart-break of women; the terror of little children, that paid for the happiness which we enjoy.

Burgoyne reached the Hudson unattacked. As he arrived, although he had no tidings from below, he heard of the successful advance in the valley of the Mohawk. St. Leger had reached Fort Stanwix without the loss of a man. It was necessary, therefore, for Burgoyne to hasten to make his junction at Albany with Howe and St. Leger, and on the 6th of August he sent word to Howe that he hoped to be in Albany by the 22d. But, even as he wrote, the blow fatal to his hopes was struck. On that very day the patriots of Tryon County, men of German blood, led by Nicholas Herkimer, were hastening to the relief of Fort Stanwix, which St. Leger had beleaguered. The tale has just been eloquently told to fifty thousand children of the Mohawk valley gathered on the field of Oriskany, and it will be told to their children's children so long as the grass of that field shall grow, and the waters of the Mohawk flow. In the hot summer morning, Herkimer and his men marched under the peaceful trees into the deadly ambush, and in the depth of the defile were suddenly enveloped in a storm of fire and death. Ah! blood-red field of Oriskany! For five doubtful desperate hours, without lines, or fort, or artillery, hand to hand, with knife and rifle, with tomahawk and spear, swaying and struggling, slipping in blood and stumbling over dead bodies, raged the most deadly battle of the war. Full of heroic deeds, full of precious memories; a sacrifice that was not lost. The stars that shone at evening over the field, saw the Indian and the white man stark and stiff, still locked in the death grapple, still clenching the hair of the foe, still holding the dripping knife in his breast. The brave Herkimer, fatally wounded, called for his Bible and tranquilly died. He did not relieve the fort, but it held out until Benedict Arnold, sent by Schuyler, coming up the valley, craftily persuaded St. Leger's Indians that his men were as the leaves of the forest for number. The savages fled; St. Leger's force melted away; the Mohawk expedition had wholly failed, and the right hand of Burgoyne was shattered.

Every day lost to the English general was now a disaster. But his fatal improvidence forced him to inaction.

He could not move without supplies of food and horses, and an expedition to secure them would also serve as a diversion to favor St. Leger. Three days after Oriskany, and before he had heard of that battle, Burgoyne detached the expedition to Bennington. New England was ready for him there as New York had been at Stanwix. Parson Allen from Pittsfield came in his chaise. Everybody else came as he could, and when the British advance was announced, John Stark marched his militia just over the line of New York, where the enemy was entrenched on the uplands of the Walloomsic, and skillfully surrounding them, the Yankee farmers who had hurried away from their summer work, swept up the hill with fiery and resistless fury, seized the blazing guns, drove the veteran troops as if they were wolves and wild cats threatening their farms, and after a lull renewing the onset against fresh foes, the New England militia won the famous battle of Bennington, and the left hand of Burgoyne was shattered.

So soon was the splendid promise of Ticonderoga darkened. The high and haughty tone was changed. "I yet do not despond," wrote Burgoyne on the 20th of August, and he had not yet heard of St. Leger's fate. But he had reason to fear. The glad light of Bennington and Oriskany had pierced the gloom that weighed upon the country. It was everywhere jubilant and everywhere rising. The savages deserted the British camp. The harvest was gathered, and while New England and New York had fallen fatally upon the flanks of Burgoyne, Washington now sent Virginia to join New York and New England in his front, detaching from his own army Morgan and his men, the most famous rifle corps of the Revolution. But while the prospect brightened, General Schuyler, by order of Congress, was superseded by General Gates. Schuyler, a most sagacious and diligent officer whom Washington wholly trusted, was removed for the alleged want of his most obvious quality, the faculty of comprehensive organization. But the New England militia disliked him, and even Samuel Adams was impatient of him; but Samuel Adams was also impatient of Washington. Public irritation with the situation, and jealous intrigue in camp and in Congress procured Schuyler's removal. He was wounded to the heart, but his patriotism did not waver. He remained in camp to be of what service he could, and he entreated Congress to order a speedy and searching inquiry into his conduct. It was at last made, and left him absolutely unstained. He was unanimously acquitted with the highest honor, and Congress approved the verdict. General Schuyler did not again enter upon active military service, but he and Rufus King were the first senators that New York sent to the Senate of the United States. Time has restored his fame, and the history of his State records no more patriotic name among her illustrious sons than that which is commemorated by this village, the name of Philip Schuyler.

Largely re-enforced, Gates, on the 12th of September, advanced to Bemis's Heights, which the young Kosciuszko had fortified, and there he awaited Burgoyne's approach. Burgoyne's orders had left him no discretion. He must force his way to Albany. With soldierly loyalty, therefore, he must assume that Howe was pushing up the Hudson, and that his own delay might imperil Howe by permitting the Americans to turn suddenly upon him. On the 11th of September he announced to his camp that he had sent the lake fleet to Canada, that he had virtually abandoned his communications, and that his army must fight its way or perish. On the 13th he crossed the Hudson, and then received his first tidings from Howe, in a letter from him written long before, and which did not even mention a junction. Burgoyne had already felt himself deserted if not betrayed, and he comprehended his critical situation. Howe was on the Delaware and Carleton would give him no aid from Canada. The country behind him was already swarming with militia. He was encamped in a dense forest, with an enemy hidden in the same forest before him, whose drumbeat and morning gun he could hear, but whose numbers and position he did not know. Yet while he could see nothing, every movement of his own was noted by an eagle eye in a tree top on the eastern side of the Hudson, and reported to Gates. And when at last Burgoyne marched out in full array, with all the glittering pomp of war, to find the foe in the forest, Gates instantly knew it. Burgoyne boldly advanced, his communication with Canada gone, the glory of Ticonderoga dimmed, the union with Howe uncertain, disaster on the right hand and on the left, the peerage and Westminster Abbey both fading from hope, and he suddenly confronted breastworks, artillery and an eager army. He must fight or fly, nor did he hesitate. At eleven o'clock on the morning of the 19th of September, he advanced in three columns towards Gates's lines on Bemis's Heights. At one o'clock the action began ; at four it was general and desperate ; at five, Burgoyne's army was in mortal peril ; at nightfall the Germans had stayed the fatal blow, and the battle ended. Both sides claimed the victory, and the British bivouacked on the field. As on Bunker Hill, the first battle in America which Burgoyne had seen, if this were a British victory another would destroy the British army.

Burgoyne huddled his dead into the ground, hastily entrenched and fortified a new position, soothed his discouraged army and meditated a fresh assault. But receiving the good news of Howe's success at the Brandywine, and of the immediate advance of Clinton to break through the highlands of the Hudson and fall upon the rear of Gates, he decided to wait. He was encamped in the wilderness without communications, but he sent word to Clinton that he could hold out until the 12th of October. Again through the forest he heard the morning and evening gun and the shouting of the American camp, and once the joyful firing of cannon that he could not understand, but which announced American victories in his rear. The alarm of the British camp was constant. The picket firing was incessant. Officers and men slept in their clothes. Rations were reduced, and the hungry army heard every night the howling of the wolves that haunted the outskirts of the camp as if making ready for their prey. At last, with provisions for sixteen days only, and no news from Clinton, Burgoyne summoned his generals for a final council. It was the evening of the 5th of October, and, could he but have known it, Howe at Germantown, had again succeeded and Sir Henry Clinton was just breaking his way through the Highlands, victorious and desolating. On the very morning that Burgoyne fought his fatal battle, the river forts had fallen, the boom and chain were cleared away, the marauding British fleet sailed into Newburgh bay, Clinton sent word gaily to Burgoyne, "Here we are! nothing between us and Albany," while Putnam was hastening up along the eastern bank and George Clinton along the western, rousing the country and rallying the flying citizens from their alarm. Of all this Burgoyne knew nothing. In his extremity, his own plan was to leave boats, provisions and magazines, for three or four days, and falling upon the left of the Americans, to attempt to gain the rear. The German General Riedesel advised falling back toward the lake. The English Fraser was willing to fight. The English Phillips was silent. Compelled to decide, Burgoyne at last determined to reconnoitre the Americans in force, and if he thought that an attack would be unwise, then to retreat toward the lake.

On the morning of the 7th of October, at 10 o'clock, fifteen hundred of the best troops in the world, led by four of the most experienced and accomplished generals, with a skirmishing van of Canadian rangers and Indians moved in three columns toward the left of the American position into a field of wheat. They began to cut forage. Startled by the rattling picket fire, the American drums beat to arms, and the British approach was announced at headquarters. Morgan and the Virginia sharp-shooters were thrown out beyond the British right. Poor, with the New York and New Hampshire men, moved steadily through the woods toward the British left, which began the battle with a vigorous cannonade. The Americans dashed forward, opened to the right and left, flanked the enemy, struck him with a blasting fire, then closed and grappling hand to hand, the mad mass of combatants swayed and staggered for half an hour, five times taking and retaking a single gun. At the first fire upon the left, the Virginia sharpshooters, shouting, and blazing with deadly aim, rushed forward with such fury that the appalled British right wavered and recoiled. While it yet staggered under the blow of Virginia, New England swept up, and with its flaming muskets broke the English line, which wildly fled. It reformed and again advanced, while the whole American force dashed against the British center, held by the Germans, whose right and left had been uncovered. The Germans bravely stood, and the British General Fraser hurried to their aid. He seemed upon the British side the inspiring genius of the day. With fatal aim an American sharpshooter fired and Fraser fell. With him sank the British heart. Three thousand New Yorkers, led by Ten Broeck, came freshly up, and the whole American line, jubilant with certain victory, advancing, Burgoyne abandoned his guns and ordered a retreat to his camp. It was but fifty-two minutes since the action began. The British dismayed, bewildered, overwhelmed, were scarcely within their redoubts, when Benedict Arnold, to whom the jealous Gates, who did not come upon the field during the day, had refused a command, outriding an aid whom Gates had sent to recall him, came spurring up;— Benedict Arnold, whose name America does not love, whose ruthless will had dragged the doomed Canadian Expedition through the starving wilderness of Maine, who volunteering to relieve Fort Stanwix had, by the mere terror of his coming, blown St. Leger away, and who, on the 19th of September, had saved the American left,—Benedict Arnold, whom battle stung to fury, now whirled from end to end of the American line, hurled it against the Great Redoubt, driving the enemy at the point of the bayonet; then flinging himself to the extreme right, and finding there the Massachusetts brigade, swept it with him to the assault, and streaming over the breastworks, scattered the Brunswickers who defended them, killed their Colonel, gained and held the point which commanded the entire British position, while at the same moment his horse was shot under him, and he sank to the ground wounded in the leg that had been wounded at Quebec. Here, upon the Hudson, where he tried to betray his country, here upon the spot where, in the crucial hour of the Revolution, he illustrated and led the American valor that made us free and great, knowing well that no earlier service can atone for a later crime, let us recall for one brief instant of infinite pity, the name that has been justly execrated for a century.

Night fell, and the weary fighters slept. Before day dawned, Burgoyne, exhausted and overwhelmed, drew off the remainder of his army, and the Americans occupied his camp. All day the lines exchanged a sharp fire. At evening, in a desolate autumn rain, having buried solemnly, amid the flash and rattle of bombs and artillery, his gallant friend, Fraser; leaving his sick and wounded to the mercies of the foe, Burgoyne who, in the splendid hour of his first advance had so proudly proclaimed "this army must not retreat," turned to fly. He moved until nearly day-break, then rested from the slow and toilsome march until toward sunset, and on the evening of the 9th crossed Fish Creek and bivouacked in the open air. A more vigorous march—but it was impracticable—would have given him the heights of Saratoga, and secured the passage of the river. But everywhere he was too late. The American sharpshooters hovered around him, cutting off supplies, and preventing him from laying roads. There was, indeed, one short hour of hope that Gates, mistaking the whole British army for its flying rear-guard, would expose himself to a destructive ambush and assault. When the snare was discovered, the last hope of Burgoyne vanished, and unable to stir, he sat down grimly north of the creek, where his army, wasted to thirty-four hundred effective men, was swiftly and completely encircled by the Americans, who commanded it at every point, and harassed it with shot and shell. Gates, with the confidence of overpowering numbers, purposely avoided battle. Burgoyne, deserted by his allies, his army half gone, with less than five days' food, with no word from Clinton, with no chance of escape, prepared honorably to surrender.

On the 14th of October, he proposed a cessation of arms to arrange terms of capitulation. His agent, Lieutenant-

Colonel Kingston, was received at the crossing of the creek by Adjutant-General Wilkinson, and was conducted by him, blindfold, to General Gates. Gates' terms required an unconditional surrender of the army as prisoners of war. Burgoyne, anxious to save his army to the king for service elsewhere, insisted that it should be returned to England, under engagement not to serve again in North America during the war. Gates had no wish to prolong the negotiations. He had heard from Putnam that the English army and fleet were triumphantly sweeping up the river, and that he must expect "the worst," and he therefore hastened to accept the proposition of Burgoyne. But Washington, with his Fabian policy, scorned even by Samuel and John Adams, had made "the worst" impossible. Hanging upon the army of Howe, engaging it, although unsuccessfully, at the Brandywine and at Germantown, he had perplexed, delayed and disconcerted the British general, gaining the time which was the supreme necessity for success against Burgoyne. By reason of Washington's operations, Howe could not strengthen Clinton as they had both expected, and Clinton could not move until his slow re-enforcements from over the sea arrived. When they came, he burst through the Highlands indeed, with fire and pillage, and hastened to fall upon the rear of Gates. But before he could reach him, while still forty miles away, he heard the astounding news of Burgoyne's surrender, and he dropped down the river sullenly, back to New York, he, too, baffled by the vigilance, the wariness, the supreme self-command of Washington.

For a moment, when Burgoyne heard of Clinton's success, he thought to avoid surrender. But it was too late. He could not, honorably, recall his word. At nine o'clock on the morning of this day, a hundred years ago, he signed the convention. At eleven o'clock his troops marched to this meadow, the site of old Fort Hardy, and with tears coursing down bearded cheeks, with passionate sobs and oaths of rage and defiance, the soldiers kissing their guns with the tenderness of lovers, or with sudden frenzy knocking off the butts of their muskets, and the drummers stamping on their drums, the King's army laid down their arms. No American eyes, except those of Morgan Lewis and James Wilkinson, aids of General Gates, beheld the surrender. As the British troops filed afterwards between the American lines, they saw no sign of exultation, but they heard the drums and fifes playing "Yankee Doodle." A few minutes later, Burgoyne and his suite rode to the headquarters of Gates. The English General, as if for a court holiday, glittered in scarlet and gold; Gates plainly clad in a blue overcoat, attended by General Schuyler in citizen's dress, who had come to congratulate him, and by his proud and happy staff, received his guest with urbane courtesy. They exchanged the compliments of soldiers. "The fortune of war, General Gates, has made me your prisoner." Gates gracefully replied, "I shall always be ready to testify that it has not been through any fault of your Excellency." The Generals entered the tent of Gates and dined together. With the same courtly compliment the English General toasted General Washington, the American General toasted the King. Then, as the English army, without artillery or arms, approached on their march to the sea, the two Generals stepped out in front of the tent, and standing together conspicuous upon this spot, in full view of the Americans and of the British army, General Burgoyne drew his sword, bowed, and presented it to General Gates. General Gates bowed, received the sword, and returned it to General Burgoyne.

Such was the simple ceremony that marked the turning point of the Revolution. All the defeats, indeed, all the struggles, the battles, the sacrifices, the sufferings, at all times and in every colony, were indispensible to the great result. Concord, Lexington, Bunker Hill, Moultrie, Long Island, Trenton, Oriskany, Bennington, the Brandywine, Germantown, Saratoga, Monmouth, Camden, Cowpen, Guilford, Eutaw Springs, Yorktown,—what American does not kindle as he calls the glorious battle roll of the revolution!—whether victories or defeats, are all essential lights and shades in the immortal picture.

But, as gratefully acknowledging the service of all the patriots, we yet call Washington father, so mindful of the value of every event, we may agree that the defeat of Burgoyne determined American independence. Thenceforth it was but a question of time. The great doubt was solved. Out of a rural militia an army could be trained to cope at every point successfully with the most experienced and disciplined troops in the world. In the first bitter moment of his defeat, Burgoyne generously wrote to a military friend, "A better armed, a better bodied, a more alert or better prepared army in all essential points of military institution, I am afraid is not to be found on our side of the question." The campaign in New York also, where the loyalists were strongest, had shown, what was afterwards constantly proved, that the British crown, despite the horrors of Cherry Valley and Wyoming, could not count upon general or effective aid from the Tories nor from the Indians. At last it was plain that if Britain would conquer, she must overrun and crush the continent, and that was impossible. The shrewdest men in England and in Europe saw it. Lord North himself, King George's chief minister, owned it, and grieved in his blind old age that he had not followed his conviction. Edmund Burke would have made peace on any terms. Charles Fox exclaimed that the ministers knew as little how to make peace as war. The Duke of Richmond urged the impossibility of conquest, and the historian Gibbon, who in Parliament had voted throughout the war as Dr. Johnson would have done, agreed that America was lost. The king of France ordered Franklin to be told that he should support the cause of the United States. In April he sent a fleet to America, and from that time to the end of the war, the French and the Americans battled together on sea and land, until on this very day, the 17th of October, 1781, four years after the disaster of Burgoyne, Cornwallis, on the plains of Yorktown, proposed a surrender to the combined armies of France and the United States. The terms were settled upon our part jointly by an American and a French officer, while Washington and La Fayette stood side by side as the British laid down their arms. It was the surrender of Burgoyne that determined the French alliance and the French alliance secured the final triumph.

It is the story of a hundred years ago. It has been ceaselessly told by sire to son, along this valley and through this land. The later attempt of the same foe and the bright day of victory at Plattsburg on the lake, renewed and confirmed the old hostility. Alienation of feeling between the parent country and the child became traditional, and on both sides of the sea a narrow prejudice survives, and still sometimes seeks to kindle the embers of that wasted fire. But here and now we stand upon the grave of old enmities. Hostile breastwork and redoubt are softly hidden under grass and grain; shot and shell and every deadly missile are long since buried deep beneath our feet, and from the mouldering dust of mingled foemen springs all the varied verdure that makes this scene so fair. While nature tenderly and swiftly repairs the ravages of war, we suffer no hostility to linger in our hearts. Two months ago the British Governor-General of Canada was invited to meet the President of the United States, at Bennington, in happy commemoration not of a British defeat but of a triumph of English liberty. So, upon this famous and decisive field, let every unworthy feeling perish! Here, to the England that we fought, let us now, grown great and strong with a hundred years, hold out the hand of fellowship and peace! Here, where the English Burgoyne, in the very moment of his bitter humiliation, generously pledged George Washington, let us, in our high hour of triumph, of power, and of hope, pledge the Queen! Here, in the grave of brave and unknown foemen, may mutual jealousies and doubts and animosities lie buried forever! Henceforth, revering their common glorious traditions, may England and America press always forward side by side, in noble and inspiring rivalry to promote the welfare of man!

Fellow-citizens, with the story of Burgoyne's surrender—the revolutionary glory of the State of New York—still fresh in our memories, amid these thousands of her sons and daughters, whose hearts glow with lofty pride, I am glad that the hallowed spot on which we stand compels us to remember not only the imperial State, but the national commonwealth whose young hands here together struck the blow, and on whose older head descends the ample benediction of the victory. On yonder height, a hundred years ago, Virginia lay encamped. Beyond, and further to the north, watched New Hampshire and Vermont. Here, in the wooded uplands at the south, stood New Jersey and New York, while across the river to the east, Connecticut and Massachusetts, closed the triumphant line. Here was the symbol of the Revolution, a common cause, a common strife, a common triumph; the cause not of a class, but of human nature—the triumph not of a colony, but of United America. And we who stand here proudly remembering—we who have seen Virginia and New York—the North and the South—more bitterly hostile than the armies whose battles shook this ground—we who have mutually proved in deadlier conflict the constancy and the courage of all the States, which, proud to be peers, yet own no master but their united selves—we renew our heart's imperishable devotion to the common American faith, the common American pride, the common American glory! Here Americans stood and triumphed. Here Americans stand and bless their memory. And here, for a thousand years, may grateful generations of Americans come to rehearse the glorious story, and to rejoice in a supreme and benignant American Nationality!

Printed by Libri Plureos GmbH in Hamburg, Germany